Alex & Jordan Design an A

Alex & Jordan Design an Adventure

The Interactive IGCSE Computer Science Pseudocode Guide

Pseudocode suitable for: *CIE iGCSE & AQA GCSE Computer Science*

Written by Holly Billinghurst

Illustrated by Seth & Holly Billinghurst

© TeachAllAboutIt Ltd. 2024 – All Rights Reserved

Alex & Jordan Design an Adventure

Holly Billinghurst is a Computer Science Teacher and tutor on the South Coast of the UK. Starting her tech career as a software developer, she fell into teaching quite by accident, but since taking her first A-level computing class back in 2009, she's never looked back.

In 2017, she founded TeachAllAboutIt. Initially as a website for her own online tutoring, since then it has expanded to include distance learning courses for home educated students, digital resources, and is where you can find her growing library of revision guides for Computer Science and Games Design.

Holly developed her online tutoring platform in response to a lack of accessible teaching and learning opportunities and it continues to be her mission to make use of technology to create an accessible & engaging classroom for all students.

In 2020, she was listed as one of '40 Women to Watch' in the digital industry and she continues to teach students online from GCSE to Higher Education while continuing to develop her e-learning platform and writing.

The characters Alex and Jordan are loosely based on her two children who both followed in Holly's footsteps and studied GCSE Computer Science. Her son now helps to illustrate the series.

Alex & Jordan Design an Adventure

Content © Copyright H A Billinghurst, 2024

Design an Adventure: The iGCSE Pseudocode Revision Book and it's contents are not endorsed by any exam board. Please refer to your exam board specification to ensure that the full range of topics has been covered.

The right of Holly Billinghurst to be identified as the author of this work has been asserted by her in accordance with the Copyright, Designs and Patents act 1988

Every reasonable effort has been made to trace copyright holder of material reproduced in this book, but if any have been inadvertently overlooked the publishers would be glad to hear from them. For legal purposes the acknowledgements throughout constitute an extension of this copyright page.

All Rights Reserved. No part of this book may be reproduced, stored in a retrieval system, or transmitted at any time or by any means mechanical, electronic, photocopying, recording, or otherwise, without the prior written permission of the publisher.

No responsibility for loss caused to any individual or organisation acting on or refraining from action as a result of the material in this publication can be accepted by the publisher or author.

A CIP record of this book is available from the British Library

First printed April 2024
ISBN: 9798322388739
Independently published by Amazon KDP

To find out more about Holly Billinghurst and this book visit
www.TeachAllAboutIT.uk

Alex & Jordan Design an Adventure

Table of Contents

What is Pseudocode Anyway? 4

Introducing Alex & Jordan 7

Part 1- Basic Elements – Input & Output 8

    Your Task: Input & Output 9

    Your Task: Input & Output (Player Data) 10

Part 2 - Selection 11

    Your Task: IF, THEN, ELSE 12

    Your Task: Choosing A Game 14

    Your Task: CASE of Snacks! 15

Part 3- Arrays &Iteration 16

    Your Task: Seating Plan List 18

    Your Task: The Dice Roll Shuffle 19

    Your Task: Voting for Games 20

    Your Task: The Scoreboard 22

    Your Task: Player Badges 24

Part 4 -Common Operators 26

    Your Task: Mini Maths Challenge 27

Part 5 -Subroutines 28

    Your Task: Maths Challenge Function 30

    Your Task: Jamie's Secret Code 31

    Your Task: The Puzzle Piece Shuffle 33

Part 6 – Searching & Sorting 34

    Your Task – Puzzling Linear Search 35

Your Task: Bubble Sort Tokens 38
Part 7 - String Operations 39
Your Task: Hidden Strings 42
Your Task: The ASCII Padlock 46
Part 8 - File Operations 47
.... 48
Your Task: Reading The Rules 48
Your Task: The Guest List 50
Extra Challenge 53
The Digital Invitation Challenge 53
Answers 56
Problem 1 – Input & Output 57
Problem 2 – Input & Output (Player Data) 59
Problem 3 – IF, THEN, ELSE 61
Problem 4 – Choosing A Game 63
Problem 5 – CASE of Snacks! 65
Problem 6 – Seating Plan List 67
Problem 7 – The Dice Roll Shuffle 69
Problem 8 – Voting for Games 71
Problem 9 – The Scoreboard 73
Problem 10 – Player Badges 75
Problem 11 – Mini Maths Challenge 78
Problem 12 – Maths Challenge Function 81
Problem 13 – Jamie's Secret Code 85

Problem 14 – The Puzzle Piece Shuffle 88

Problem 15 – Puzzling Linear Search 91

Problem 16 – Bubble Sort Tokens 94

Problem 17 – Hidden Strings 96

Problem 18 – The ASCII Padlock 98

Problem 19 – Reading The Rules.............................. 101

Problem 20 – The Guest List..................................... 103

Extra Challenge Solution: 105

The Digital Invitation Challenge 105

More Books by The Author 108

What is Pseudocode Anyway?

Have you ever tried to explain how to make a sandwich to a friend, where you go step by step through the process without worrying about the brand of bread or whether the mayo should be light or not in there at all? That's kind of what pseudocode is like for computers. It's a way to jot down how to solve a problem step by step, without getting tangled up in the specifics of a programming language like Python or Java.

So, What Exactly Is Pseudocode?

Imagine you've got a brilliant idea for a program, something that could remind you to water your plants or maybe even help with your homework. But this idea is just floating around in your head, and you need to make it clear not only to yourself but also to others (or perhaps later a computer) how it should work. This is where pseudocode comes into play. Pseudocode is like a draft, or an outline of a program written in plain language that humans can understand. It uses a mix of common words and some programming terms to describe the steps your program should take.

If we remember that an algorithm is a set of steps that shows how to solve a problem or reach a goal, we can see that pseudocode is just a text version of an algorithm.

The beauty of pseudocode is that it's not written in any specific programming language. It's a *high-level description*, which means it focuses on the big picture of what your program will do without getting bogged down in the details of syntax[1] rules that actual coding languages have.

So Why Do We Use Pseudocode?

You might be wondering, *"If pseudocode isn't real code, why bother with it?"* Well, there are a few good reasons:

Planning Ahead

Before architects build a house, they draw a blueprint. Pseudocode is like a blueprint for your program. It helps you organize your thoughts and the steps needed to make your program work before diving into the actual coding, which saves you a ton of time and headaches later.

Communication

Not everyone programs in Python or JavaScript (*or any other specific language*), but most programmers can understand pseudocode. It's a universal way of describing your program's logic to teachers, examiners, or even developers who use different programming languages.

It's all about making sure everyone's on the same page.

---

[1] Syntax – the spelling & grammar of a language

Problem-Solving

Sometimes, coding can feel like trying to solve a puzzle with a million pieces. Pseudocode helps you focus on solving the problem step by step, rather than getting stuck on a specific code syntax or bug.

Exam Practice

For the Cambridge International iGCSE Computer Science exams, you'll be asked to use a combination of pseudocode, program code, and flowcharts to show how you'd solve programming problems. Missing one of these three skills will make the exam much harder!

Pseudocode is your first step in turning a brilliant program idea into reality. It's about making complex problems simpler and ensuring that everyone, from you in the future to seasoned developers, can understand what you're trying to achieve.

To help you along the way, you can access detailed learning content for each section in the TeachAllAboutIt iGCSE Computer Science online courses. The course is packed with explanations, videos, and practice questions designed to reinforce your learning and prepare you for your exams.

Introducing Alex & Jordan

Alex and Jordan are friends who both study Computer Science together. They use their computational thinking skills to make their life easier, but also to help solve problems in the world around them.

Alex is an adventurer, always planning new things for them to do and enjoys creating games for their friends to play together.

Jordan is a little more relaxed, and enjoys reading and takes a little more time to think through problems, breaking them down until they understand them.

As you read through this book, you'll be working through a set of logic puzzles to solve with pseudocode, helping both of them to plan and run a games evening with their friends. There'll be problems for you to solve from invitation lists to creating treasure hunt games for the group to play.

You'll need a pen & paper, but if you need a helping hand, the answers and explanations are included in the book!

Part 1- Basic Elements - Input & Output

For our first problem, we're starting with the basics of declaring variables and handling input/output operations. Remember, variables are like containers in programming, storing information that your program can then manipulate.

Alex and Jordan have decided to plan a board game night and want to create a simple program to manage their guest list and the games they'll play. They've decided to start by creating a program that asks for a friend's name and their favourite board game. This information will then be stored and used later to organize the event.

Syntax Reminder

At the start of each section, you'll see a syntax reminder to show you the style and layout of each statement.

Declaration (Creating a variable)
```
DECLARE <identifier> : <data type>
```

Assignment (giving a variable a value)
```
<identifier> ← <value>
```

Input/Output
```
INPUT <identifier>
OUTPUT <value(s)>
```

Alex & Jordan Design an Adventure

Your Task: Input & Output

Write the pseudocode to:

- **Declare** two variables: one for storing a friend's name and another for their favourite board game.
- **Prompt** Alex and Jordan to enter their friend's name and then their favourite game.
- **Output** a message that confirms the friend's name and their favourite game have been recorded.

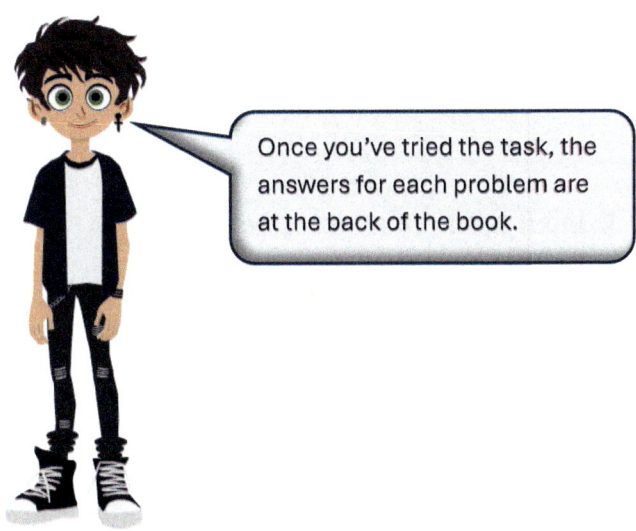

Once you've tried the task, the answers for each problem are at the back of the book.

Now that they've seen logic can help them make lasts easier, the friends decide to gather more detailed preferences from their friends to ensure everyone has a great time. They want to create a program that collects information on how many games each friend wishes to play and whether they prefer strategy games or chance games.

Alex & Jordan Design an Adventure

Alex has started reaching out to their friendship group to ask about their preferences for the upcoming board game night. Jodan suggests that they should create a program that will ask each person for their name, how many games they'd like to play, and whether they prefer strategy or chance games.

They record everything into their planner but need something more high-tech to help them identify which game to choose.

Your Task: Input & Output (Player Data)

Write the pseudocode to:

- **Prompt** the user to enter the name of their friend.
- **Ask** how many games their friend wants to play.
- **Ask** whether their friend prefers strategy games or chance games.
- **Output** a message that shows the friend's preferences, including their name, the number of games they wish to play, and their game preference.

Part 2 - Selection

Alex and Jordan are thrilled with the progress they've made on their board game night program. As it's going so well, they decide to add a feature to recommend a game based on the number of players. They'd love to play Galactic Defenders, but it's only for groups of 4 or more, so they need a different recommendation for smaller groups.

To solve this problem, they'll need to use **selective statements**. Your task is to help them write the pseudocode that includes a basic selection structure using IF and ELSE to make this decision.

```
Syntax Reminder

Logical Operators
= equal to
< less than
<= less than or equal to
> greater than
>= greater than or equal to
<> not equal to

IF Statements
IF <condition>
 THEN
  <statements>
  ELSE
  <statements>
ENDIF
```

The program will need to ask the user for the number of players planning to play. If the number is 4 or more, the program should recommend a game designed for larger groups. Otherwise, it should suggest a different game suitable for 2-3 players.

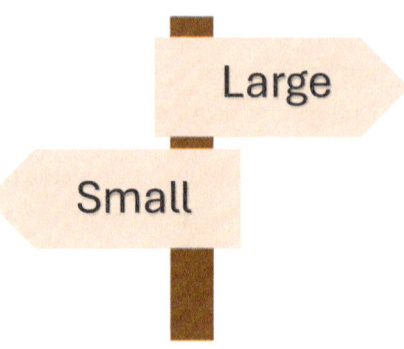

Your Task: IF, THEN, ELSE

Write the pseudocode to:

- **Prompts** the user to enter the number of players.
- Uses an **IF statement** to check if the number of players is 4 or more. If so, the program should output a message recommending "Galactic Defenders".
- **IF** the number of players is less than 4, the **ELSE** part of the statement should suggest playing "Mystery Mansion".
- **Outputs** the appropriate game recommendation based on the number of players.

Remember, the aim is to practice using IF and ELSE statements to make decisions within your pseudocode.

Alex & Jordan Design an Adventure

Alex and Jordan are excited about their upcoming game night, but they realize that with a variety of friends coming over who might want to play in smaller groups, they need a more complex approach to game recommendations. They decide to categorise their game recommendations based on the exact number of players, offering a different suggestion for each possible group size.

The friends have four games in mind, each best suited for a different number of players. They need a program that recommends a game based on whether their group will have 2, 3, 4, or more than 4 players.

2 players: "Puzzle Quest"

3 players: "Mystery Mansion"

4 players: "Galactic Defenders"

More than 4 players: "Empire Builders"

Your task is to help Alex and Jordan by writing pseudocode that uses IF, ELSE IF, and ELSE to make these recommendations based on the user's input.

Alex & Jordan Design an Adventure

Your Task: Choosing A Game

Write the pseudocode that:

- **Asks** the user for the number of players.
- Uses **selection** to recommend a game:
    - *If the number is 2, suggest "Puzzle Quest".*
    - *Otherwise if the number is 3, suggest "Mystery Mansion".*
    - *Otherwise if the number is 4, suggest "Galactic Defenders".*
    - *Finally, for any number greater than 4, suggest "Empire Builders".*
- **Outputs** the game recommendation based on the number of players.

Jordan is getting everything ready for their game night when Alex reminds them that no game night is complete without the perfect selection of snacks! They decide to improve their program by suggesting a snack based on the game being played because all good games deserve snacks.

Alex & Jordan Design an Adventure

They select four games and a corresponding snack for each:

"Puzzle Quest": Popcorn

"Mystery Mansion": Chocolate Chip Cookies

"Galactic Defenders": Pizza

"Empire Builders": Pretzels

Your task is to help them write pseudocode that uses a CASE statement to recommend a snack based on the user's choice of game.

Syntax Reminder

Case Statements
```
CASE OF <IDENTIFIER>
   "value 1" : "statement"
   "value 2" : "statement"
   ...
ENDCASE
```

Your Task: CASE of Snacks!

Write the pseudocode to:

- **Prompts** the user to **input** the name of the game they've chosen for the evening.
- Uses a **CASE statement** to select and recommend a snack that pairs well with the chosen game.
- **Outputs** the snack recommendation.

Part 3- Arrays & Iteration

As the game night approaches, the friends realize they have another important aspect to work out - the seating arrangement! With four friends coming over, they want everyone to feel included and use the seating setup as part of the games – not musical chairs, but swapping seats nonetheless.

After some thought, they decided to use their growing programming skills to create a seating chart and save it as a list.

Their friends, Taylor, Morgan, Casey, and Jamie are just as excited about the evening. As they arrive, Alex thinks it would be fun to assign seats around the gaming table in a way that mixes everyone up, giving them a chance to catch up and share laughs, no matter the game being played. Interested to see where this will go, Jordan assigns everyone their seats around the table.

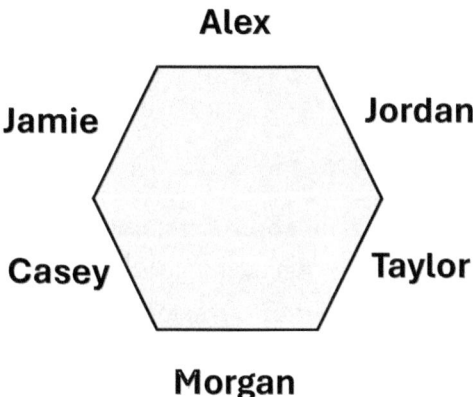

Alex & Jordan Design an Adventure

```
Syntax Reminder

Declaring Arrays
DECLARE <identifier> : ARRAY[<l>:<u>] OF <data
type>

Assigning to Arrays
StudentNames[1] ← "Ali"

Count Controlled Iteration (FOR Loop)
FOR <identifier> ← <value1> TO <value2>
 <statements>
NEXT <identifier>
```

Your task is to help Alex and Jordan write pseudocode that uses a 1D array to store the names of all the people attending the games night, including themselves, and a FOR loop to display the seating order around the table.

Hint: *think about each of the chairs around the table being lined up in order to form the array.*

Your Task: Seating Plan List

Write the pseudocode to:

- **Declare** a 1D array containing the names of Alex, Jordan, and their four friends.
- Uses a **FOR loop** to go through the array
- **Output** each person's name along with their seat number around the table.

As the game night is in full swing, Jordan introduces a fun twist to keep things interesting.

Between games, they propose adding a mini-game where each player can roll a 6-sided dice to determine how many seats they will move clockwise around the table.

This playful challenge is agreed upon by all of the friends, as it promises to add an element of surprise and ensures everyone gets to spend time with each other throughout the evening.

Your task is to help Alex and Jordan modify their seating arrangement program to include the ability to tell the players what seat they should move to.

The program should allow the player in seat 0 to 'roll' the dice and then all players will move the specified number of seats clockwise.

Alex & Jordan Design an Adventure

```
Syntax Reminder

Creating Random Numbers
Value ← ROUND(RANDOM() * <max integer>, <places>)
```

Your Task: The Dice Roll Shuffle

Write the pseudocode to:

- Simulate a dice roll using a **random number.**
- **Calculate** the new seating arrangement after all players move the specified number of seats clockwise using an array.
- **Output** the new seating arrangement showing the name & new seat number.

The "Dice Roll Shuffle," proves to work well, and now they've played a few games, Alex suggests introducing another interactive element to their game night: a secret vote to choose the next game. Although Jordan was hoping that they could play one of their own games, the friends all agree that instead of openly discussing and deciding on the next game, each player will cast a vote, and the game with the most votes will be next to be played.

To make this process fair, Jordan suggests a plan to use two parallel 1D arrays: one to store the names of the games being voted on and another to count the votes each game receives. The data at each index of the arrays will correspond to the other.

Your task is to help Alex and Jordan set up the secret vote system in their program. The program will track the games available for voting and count the votes each game receives. As you look around the room, you see that there are **4 games** to choose from and **6 players** voting.

Your Task: Voting for Games

Write the pseudocode to:

- **Hold** a list of games and their corresponding votes in two parallel 1D arrays.
- **Output** game options to choose from.
- Allow each player to **input** a vote for their preferred game.
- **Calculate** the game with the most votes.
- **Output** the winning game.

As the "Secret Vote" game is played, and the "Dice Roll Shuffle" keeps everyone moving, Alex and Jordan's game night is in full swing.

As the games continue, they realized they need a way to keep track of everyone's scores across different games to add a bit of competitiveness to the group, and to identify the overall winner at the end of the night. After all, the winner gets cake... maybe.

To do this, the friends decide to introduce a scoreboard that can track each player's score for each game played. Understanding that this requires storing more complex data, they decide to use a 2D array, which is similar to a table of data, allowing them to organize scores by player and game.

Your task is to help Alex and Jordan set up a scoreboard using a 2D array. This scoreboard will keep track of each player's scores across different games with a row for each player and columns for their name and score for each game.

Using a 2D Array

Syntax:
```
<identifier> ← [[<item>,<item>],[<item>,<item>]]
```

A 2D array is set up like an array of arrays. Each row is a smaller array that holds the data items (columns) for that row.

Alex & Jordan Design an Adventure

Your Task: The Scoreboard

Write the pseudocode that:

- Uses a **2D array** to hold scores for each player across four games.
- **Stores** the scores using the following table of data:

	Game 1	Game 2	Game 3	Game 4
Alex	5	8	7	6
Jordan	3	5	2	9
Taylor	4	6	8	2
Morgan	5	3	7	5
Casey	4	6	9	2
Jamie	8	4	2	8

- **Calculates** the total score for each player.
- **Outputs** the score in a user-friendly format.

After keeping score across various games, Alex and Jordan realize they could make things more exciting for everyone by introducing a leaderboard. This will not only track scores but also add badges next to each player's name based on their ranking—something fun to aim for beyond just winning individual games.

To make this work, they'll need to track not only the scores but also the badges in a parallel 1D array, with each badge title corresponding to the player's position in the scores array.

Alex & Jordan Design an Adventure

Parallel Arrays

Because arrays use indexes to access their data, this means that more than one array can be used together as long as the data at each position matches.

In the tables below, the data in the first array matches the data at the same position in the second array. This means they are in parallel.

[0]	[1]	[2]
Bugs	Peter	Tom

[0]	[1]	[2]
Bunny	Rabbit	Kitten

Your task is to help Alex and Jordan set up a leaderboard that uses a 2D array for scores and a 1D array for badges.

Alex & Jordan Design an Adventure

Your Task: Player Badges

Write the pseudocode to:

- Use the **same 2D array** called Scoreboard as before to store the game scores for each player. You can assume that this is already defined and contains the data below:

	Game 1	Game 2	Game 3	Game 4
Alex	5	8	7	6
Jordan	3	5	2	9
Taylor	4	6	8	2
Morgan	5	3	7	5
Casey	4	6	9	2
Jamie	8	4	2	8

- Use a **parallel 1D array** to assign the players' badges:
    - If a player's total is 40, their badge is "perfectionist"
    - If a player's total is more than 20, then their badge is "Strategist"
    - If a player's total is more than 10, then their badge is "Optimist"
    - Otherwise, their badge is "Newbie"
- **Output** each player's name, their total score, and their badge.

Constructs

Most programming languages are created using a set of constructs. These act like the building blocks for the program, and these have been the basic blocks that you have used so far.

Sequence:
Just like a sequence of numbers or letters, sequence in programming identifies the order in which the lines of code run.

Selection:
Selective statements run blocks of code only if a condition is true. IF statements and CASE statements are both types of selection.

Iteration:
Iterate, in Latin, means "repeat" so iterative statements in programming create loops in the code where blocks of code are repeated *(so we don't need to write the code many times. Phew!).*

Count-controlled iteration repeats a set number of times and includes a special variable that counts how many times the loop has run.

Condition-controlled iteration will keep repeating until a condition is met (possibly infinitely!)

Part 4 - Common Operators

As the scoreboard is put up and everyone is keen to start competing for badges, Alex and Jordan decide to create a mini game for their friends to play between board games.

They call it the "Mini-Maths Challenge." The idea is simple: each player will roll two 6-sided dice. The first roll will determine the number of points to start with.

The second roll will dictate the number of points to add, subtract, multiply, or divide by, depending on the outcome of a spinner with options for each mathematical operation.

There's just one small problem – Alex is having a tough time remembering and calculating all the numbers that the friends are rolling with their dice and shouting. It's all too much!

STOP!!

Jordan suggests that they stick with their idea of a maths challenge, but use a program to generate, store, and calculate the answers. After all, learning to program is also about learning to get the computer to do the hard work for you!

Now that they're agreed to use a computer program, Jordan suggests adding a twist. If the spinner lands on a special section, the points will either be divided by the dice roll using integer division (DIV) or the remainder will be taken (MOD).

MOD & DIV

DIV is used for Integer division, or how many times does x go into y?

11 DIV 2 = 5

MOD is the modulo. This is the name for the remainder after division.

11 MOD 2 = 1

Your task is to help Alex and Jordan program the Mini-Maths Challenge. The program should simulate rolling dice, spinning the spinner, and performing the mathematical operation on the points.

Your Task: Mini Maths Challenge

Write the pseudocode that:

- **Simulates** a player rolling two 6-sided dice.
- Generates a 'spinner' to randomly select a **mathematical operation** (+, -, *, /, DIV, MOD).
- Applies the operation to the first and second dice roll.
- **Outputs** the dice rolls, the operation, and the final score in a user friendly format.

Part 5 - Subroutines

As the night progresses, Alex and Jordan notice that running the "Mini-Maths Challenge" was a hit, but it was a bit repetitive to manage. To make the process easier and more efficient, they decide to use subroutines in their program.

A subroutine is like a mini program within a program that can be used over and over again. They know that this will not only save time but also make it easier to play the mini-game multiple times throughout the night.

Syntax Reminder

Procedure: a subroutine that doesn't return a value
Function: a subroutine that returns a value

Defining Procedures
```
PROCEDURE <identifier>(<param1>:<datatype>,…)
  <statements>
ENDPROCEDURE
```

Calling Procedures
```
CALL <identifier>(Value1,...)
```

Alex suggests that they take their maths challenge program apart and look for areas that are similar or repeated that could be tidied away into their own named block of code.

They decide that the best part of the code to be tidied away is the calculations. Their subroutine will act like a magical maths box with numbers being fed in and whole calculations be sent back out!

Who knows what goes on inside the maths function box… well, Alex and Jordan do! (*they designed it*)

Your task is to help Alex and Jordan create a subroutine in their program that can be called each time they want to perform the "Mini-Maths Challenge."

Your Task: Maths Challenge Function

Write the pseudocode to:

- **Simulate** the same dice rolls and mathematical operation of the "Mini-Maths Challenge."
- Passes in the two dice rolls as **parameters** into a procedure called `PerformMathsChallenge`
- The procedure will:
    - **Calculate** the a value using a random operation and the two integers.
    - **Output** the result of the calculation.

Feeling pleased with the games and puzzles that they have created so far, Alex and Jordan begin to plan a grand finale for their game night – a treasure hunt for all the friends called "The Quest for the Golden Token".

To make it more exciting, Jamie suggests that they create a challenge that requires players to crack a code to reveal the hiding spot. They decide to use a function in their program to calculate a secret code based on players' inputs.

Syntax Reminder

Defining Functions
```
FUNCTION <identifier>(<param1>:<datatype>,…)
RETURNS <data type>
 <statements>
FUNCTION
```

Calling Functions
```
<variable> ← <identifier>(Value1,...)
```

Alex & Jordan Design an Adventure

Your task is to help Alex and Jordan create a function that will implement Jamie's idea of a secret code. Players will input two numbers, and the function will perform operations on these numbers to output the secret code.

Your Task: Jamie's Secret Code

Write the pseudocode to create a function that:

1. Takes two integers as **inputs**.
2. **Multiplies** the first number by 3.
3. **Adds** the second number to the result from step 2.
4. **Divides** the total by 2 to get the secret code.
5. **Returns** the secret code.

Alex & Jordan Design an Adventure

With the secret code cracked and the Golden Token found, Alex and Jordan want to keep the momentum going. Out of ideas, Casey suggests that they design another challenge called "The Puzzle Piece Shuffle."

In this game, each player will receive a set of numbered puzzle pieces, and they would use a function in their program to shuffle the pieces. The goal was for each player to then arrange their shuffled pieces in the correct order.

Your task is to help Alex and Jordan create a function that shuffles an array of puzzle pieces.

Each player will use this function to get their starting pieces which will be already shuffled!

Syntax Reminder

Assigning to Arrays
`<identifier>[<index>] ← <Value>`

Getting Data from Arrays
`<Value> ← <identifier>[<index>]`

Your Task: The Puzzle Piece Shuffle

Write the pseudocode to create a function that:

- Accepts an **array of integers** as its parameter.
- Shuffles the array using a **swapping algorithm**.
- **Returns** the shuffled array.

Outside the function, **iterate** through the returned array to output the shuffled puzzle pieces for a player.

Shuffling Data

There are many different ways to shuffle data, but the most human way to do this is to pick two items at random and swap them, then repeat this a random number of times.

Swapping Data

A computer can only move one piece of data at a time, so swapping uses three steps.

Step 1: *put the 1st item into a temporary variable*
temp ← array[a]

Step 2: *put the 2nd item into the 1st item's place*
array[a] ← array[b]

Step 3: *put the temporary variable into the 2nd item's place*
array[b] ← temp

Part 6 - Searching & Sorting

After the excitement of "The Puzzle Piece Shuffle," Alex and Jordan notice that something is amiss. In the chaos of shuffling, one of the Golden Token puzzle pieces had mysteriously disappeared, turning their game night into a real-life mystery adventure!

To find the missing piece quickly, they decide to use their programming skills once more, this time using a linear search algorithm. The friends gather all the puzzle pieces, number them, and prepare to search through them one by one in turn.

> **Standard Algorithm - Linear Search**
>
> Linear search is one of the simplest searching algorithms. It works by looking at each item in a list or array one by one until the desired item is found or the list ends. This method is useful as it doesn't require the data to be sorted but can take a long time if there is a lot of data.
>
> Imagine you have a small box filled with coloured balls, each marked with a number:
> [4, 1, 5, 3, 2].
> You want to find the ball marked with the number 3.
>
> **First ball** = 4. Not a match, move to the next.
> **Second ball** = 1. It's still not a match, move on.
> **Third ball** = 5. Not yet, keep going.
> **Fourth ball** = 3. You've found a match!

Morgan is confused as she takes her turn to search through the pieces. She's looked through each spot in turn and still hasn't found the missing piece! Alex explains that if she's got to the end of the list, then the piece can't be there, and it's time to stop.

Your task is to help Alex and Jordan write a pseudocode program that implements a linear search to find the missing puzzle piece.

Your Task – Puzzling Linear Search

Write the pseudocode for a program that:

- **Stores** an array of puzzle pieces, each identified by a unique number.
- Uses a **linear search** to find a specific puzzle piece number input by the user.
- **Outputs** whether the piece is found and its position in the array.
- If the puzzle piece isn't in the list, a suitable message is **output**.

Alex & Jordan Design an Adventure

Finally, the missing puzzle piece is found under the table where Casey had been juggling! Now that the game can be put away, Jordan suggests a new game to keep the friends working together. They call it "The Great Sort-Out Challenge". Jordan explains that this isn't a trick to get them tidying up, but instead a logic game for them to play.

They hand out a jumbled collection of numbered tokens to each friend and start to explain the challenge. Each friend must sort the tokens into ascending order as quickly as possible using simple instructions that a computer would understand.

To make sure that everyone uses a standard set of instructions, Alex suggests that they simulate the sorting process called Bubble Sort algorithm.

Alex points to the fizzy drinks on the table and explains that Bubble Sort uses a process that bubbles the largest numbers to the top, just like the largest bubbles in the glasses are floating to the top of the drink!

Jordan agrees that this is a fair way for the friends to solve the puzzle and suggests that they all try to work out a way to sort the tokens using this as a

Standard Algorithm - Bubble Sort

Bubble Sort is a sorting algorithm that repeatedly steps through a list, comparing items in pairs. As it checks each pair, if they are in the wrong order, it swaps them. The process is repeated until the list is sorted. Each time the whole list is checked through, this is called a **Pass**.

The name "Bubble Sort" comes from the way larger items "bubble" to the top of the list (*end of the array*) as the sorting progresses, just as air bubbles rise through water.

Imagine you were sorting this list of numbers: [5, 3, 8, 4, 2]

First Pass:
Compare 5 and 3. Since 5 > 3, swap them. List now: [3, 5, 8, 4, 2]
Compare 5 and 8. Since 5 < 8, do nothing. List remains: [3, 5, 8, 4, 2]
Compare 8 and 4. Since 8 > 4, swap them. List now: [3, 5, 4, 8, 2]
Compare 8 and 2. Since 8 > 2, swap them. List now: [3, 5, 4, 2, 8]

Second Pass:
Compare 3 and 5. Since 5 > 3, do nothing. List remains: [3, 5, 4, 2, 8]
Compare 5 and 4. Since 5 > 4, swap them. List now: [3, 4, 5, 2, 8]

> Compare 5 and 2. Since 5 > 2, swap them. List now: [3, 4, 2, 5, 8]
> Compare 5 and 8. Since 8 > 5, do nothing. List remains: [3, 4, 2, 5, 8]
>
> **Additional Passes:**
> As there were swaps made in the previous pass, keep repeating this process until a full pass is made where no swaps happen. This means that the list is sorted:
> [2, 3, 4, 5, 8]
>
> Bubble Sort is best suited for *small lists* as it is inefficient on large lists compared to more advanced sorting algorithms like Merge Sort or Quick Sort because of the number of loops needed to get the data in order.

Your task is to help the friends create a program that uses Bubble Sort to arrange a series of numbers in ascending order (low to high).

Your Task: Bubble Sort Tokens

Write the pseudocode for a program that:

- **Stores** an array of unordered numbers representing the tokens.
- Uses **Bubble Sort** to sort the array in ascending order and uses a **flag** variable to stop the algorithm.
- **Outputs** the sorted array.

Alex & Jordan Design an Adventure

Part 7 - String Operations

By now, the friends are enjoying using their computational thinking skills to create their own games, but they want to try something more detailed than just maths calculations or sorting out jumbled data.

For their next game, they decide to work together to plan a treasure hunt with a twist. Instead of simply searching for clues, the clues will be hidden in notes written to contain secret messages.

Each note will hold a string of letters, but the actual clue will be embedded as a set of **substrings** inside each note.

To decipher the clues, players must extract the substrings using a set of numbers that tell them the positions and lengths of each word. They will then need to piece them together to find the next clue's location.

> **Syntax Reminder**
>
> **Getting the Length of a String**
> LENGTH(<identifier>)
>
> **Getting a Substring of a String**
> SUBSTRING(<identifier>, <start>, <length>)
>
> *Generally, when we use a Substring function, the start position of the first character in the string is 1 (unlike arrays where it is 0).*

Alex explains to the friends that they could imagine a string as a sequence of characters, like a sentence or a word. A substring is then any consecutive sequence of characters taken from this string.

Taylor looks a bit confused by this, so Alex describes how they used a substring and some string manipulation to create a nickname for Jordan.

Alex tells Taylor that Jordan's name is a string: "Jordan", and they can extract a part of this string as a nickname.

Alex shows the friends how they used the SUBSTRING function on Jordan's name:

The String: "Jordan"

Goal: Extract the substring "Dan" from "Jordan".

The Code: SUBSTRING("Jordan", 4, 3)

> The SUBSTRING function that Alex uses tells the program:
>
> *Start at the 4th character of the string "Jordan" (which is "d").*
>
> *Extract 3 characters from this position onwards ("dan").*
>
> *They could also use the function UCASE() on the first letter to make this a capital letter as it's a name.*
>
> *So, Alex's program might look like this:*
>
> Name = "Jordan"
> Nickname = SUBSTRING(Name,4,1).UCASE()
> Nickname = Nickname + SUBSTRING(Name,5,2)
>
> OUTPUT Nickname
>
> *This would output the string "Dan".*

Now that they understand how substrings can be extracted from longer strings, the friends all get to work creating a set of secret clues for the game.

Their notes include a long string at the start made up of the words for their clue, and other random characters. After each hidden clue is a set of numbers giving the starting location of each word in the string and how long the string is.

Your task is to help the friends write a program that extracts the hidden clues from their secret notes using string operations.

> **Syntax Reminder**
>
> There are two other useful substring functions that can be used to extract characters from the beginning and end of strings.
>
> `LEFT(<identifier>,<length>)`
> Gets a set number of characters from the start of a string.
>
> `RIGHT(<identifier>,<length>)`
> Gets a set number of characters from the end of a string.

Your Task: Hidden Strings

Write the pseudocode for a program that:

- **Stores** a series of secret notes as strings:
- Uses the **SUBSTRING** function to extract parts of the notes based on these clues (the first note parts are below):
- **Outputs** the substrings to reveal the hidden clues.

Alex & Jordan Design an Adventure

Clue 1

"X7bQTheX5firstX2clueX9isX4nearX8theX6oldX3oakX1tree."

[[5,3],[10,5],[17,4],[23,2], [27,4],[33,3],[38,3], [43,3],[48,4]]

Clue 2

"FindX3theX4secondX2clueX1underX5theX6stoneX7bench."

[[1,4], [7,3], [12,6], [20,4], [26,5], [33,3],[38,5], [45,5]]

Clue 3

"TheX1lastX4clueX3isX2hiddenX5inX6theX7gardenX8shed."

[[1,3], [6,4], [12,4], [18,2], [22,6], [30,2], [34,3], [39,6], [47,4]]

Jamie shouts out to the others as they crack the code and run to the final hiding place but discover that Alex and Jordan have already thought ahead! As Jamie reaches the shed door, they see it's locked with a four-number padlock.

They try a few combinations using numbers that might mean something to either Alex or Jordan, but the lock won't budge.

Jamie tells the others what they've found, and they try some of the other patterns that they've learnt through the evening, like putting the numbers in order and looking for number clues in the notes.

As Jordan catches up to the group, they explain that trying to crack the lock using brute force will take them far too long. Worried that they'd done something wrong, Jamie tells Jordan that they weren't trying to break the lock!

Jordan tells Jamie not to worry, and that brute force in computing means to try every possible combination instead of calculating a solution. They laugh and explain that a lock with just four digits can have up to ten thousand different combinations, which might take Jamie some time!

Alex explains to the friends that this is actually the final challenge of the treasure hunt: the ASCII Code Lock Challenge.

Alex & Jordan Design an Adventure

In this final part of the game, the friends need to discover a word hidden within a riddle. To win the game and open the lock, they must convert the characters of the word into their ASCII values.

With a grin, Alex explains that they wouldn't make it as simple as that to win the game! The twist in the problem is that characters in the word in an even position, must be converted to the uppercase version of their ASCII number, and those in an odd position will use the lowercase ASCII number.

> **ASCII Characters**
>
> The ASCII character set assigns a number to each character you see on your keyboard. Upper-case and lower-case letters are given different numbers to allow the computer to tell them apart.
>
> In ASCII, Alex's name could be converted to:
>
> A = 65   l = 108   e = 101   x = 120

Casey thinks about this and asks how they would find just four digits from these numbers when ASCII letters have 2 or more digits each.

Alex explains that the digits of the numbers that each character is converted to must be added together until the result is just one digit.

The final four numbers created by this algorithm will be the combination to the padlock guarding the winner's treasure (*even if that is just chocolate bars and the winner's badge*).

Syntax Reminder

Converting to Upper Case
UCASE(<identifier>)

Converting to Lower Case
LCASE(<identifier>)

Converting to an ASCII Number
ORD(<identifier>)

Your task is to help Jamie create a program that converts a word into the padlock combination:

Your Task: The ASCII Padlock

Write the pseudocode for a program that:

- Accepts a 4 letter word as **input**.
- Checks the substring **position** of each letter.
    - **If even**, convert the character to **uppercase**.
    - **If odd**, convert the character to **lowercase**.
- **Converts** each letter into its **ASCII number**.
- For each converted number, **adds the digits** together until there is only **one digit**.
- **Outputs** the four-digit code as the padlock combination.

Part 8 - File Operations

The friends decide to end the evening with a quieter, but longer board game. As they set out their pieces on the table a huge rule book drops out of the box. Everyone winces at the size of the rule book and begin to debate who should be the one to read the rules out.

Jordan wonders if, instead of reading, they could use their programming skills to create a file for the computer to read out to them.

They check their laptop, and it can indeed read aloud, but only if the data is saved in a text file and output to the screen.

Jordan creates a new text file on their laptop and names it "UltimateGameRules.txt". Using the online copy of the rules, Jordan pastes in the text, but is unsure how to get the text from the file out to the screen.

Your task is to help Jordan write a program that reads the rules of the next game from the text file and display them on the screen so the digital reader can read the rules to the friends.

> **Syntax Reminder**
>
> **Opening a Text File**
> OPENFILE <File identifier> FOR <File mode>
> File mode can be READ or WRITE
>
> **Read a Line of a File**
> READFILE <File Identifier>, <Variable>
>
> **Close a Text File**
> CLOSEFILE <File identifier>

Your Task: Reading The Rules

Write the pseudocode for a program that:

- **Opens** a text file named "UltimateGameRules.txt" for reading.
- **Reads** each line of the file and **stores** it in a variable.
- **Outputs** each line to display the rules of the game.
- **Closes** the file after reading all the content.

Alex & Jordan Design an Adventure

As the final game of the night draws to a close, Alex, Jordan, and their friends agree that they've had a great time with each other.

However, they have one last challenge for their friends - a document to remember the evening they'd shared and the problems that they've solved together.

To keep a record of the evening with their friends, Alex and Jordan decide to return to their very first challenge and create a digital guest list that captures the names of all those who have joined them in their adventure.

This guest list will not only be a keepsake for everyone but also an invitation to future game nights!

Alex
Jamie
Morgan
Casey
Taylor
Jordan

Alex & Jordan Design an Adventure

Your task is to help Alex and Jordan write a program that creates a digital guest list by saving the names of all attendees to a text file named "CelebrationGuestList.txt".

> **Syntax Reminder**
>
> **Writing a Line To a File**
> WRITEFILE <File identifier>, <Variable>
>
> **Close a Text File**
> CLOSEFILE <File identifier>

Your Task: The Guest List

Write the pseudocode for a program that:

- **Opens** a new text file named "CelebrationGuestList.txt" for **writing**.
- Prompts Alex and Jordan to **input** each guest's name, one at a time, and **writes** each name to the file.
- **Continues** accepting names **until** they decide to stop by inputting a specific keyword, such as "END".
- **Closes** and saves the file.

As the evening's laughter and excitement gently settle and each of the guests goes home, Alex and Jordan gather around the soft glow of their computer screen, the digital guest list before them—a roster of adventurers, thinkers, and code breakers who had joined them on an unforgettable adventure.

Alex & Jordan Design an Adventure

They look towards you, a smile on their faces, and wish you a heartfelt thanks.

"We couldn't have done this without you," Alex says, their eyes reflecting the screen's light. "Every puzzle is solved, every code is cracked, and every challenge overcome was thanks to your guidance and creativity."

Jordan nods in agreement. "This adventure - our game night - has been something we've wanted to do for ages but could never quite work out how. You've been part of this story, an unseen friend guiding us through each twist and turn."

Once alive with the sounds of shared challenges and victories, the living room has quieted down, but the air is still charged with the buzz of all the challenges.

"As we end this time together," Jordan continues, "we're excited about what lies ahead. We've learnt so much about logic and planning, but this is really just the beginning."

Alex agrees and adds, "So, from the bottom of our hearts, thank you for being part of our journey. Our adventure was brighter with your help, and we can't wait to see where we'll go next, together."

As the final screen dims, Alex and Jordan head to bed, their thoughts already racing with ideas for the next game night. This was more than a sneaky way to code with their friends; it was a celebration of the endless possibilities when you think with logic and creativity combined.

And you, reader, were at the heart of it all. Thank you for joining all of us on this adventure. Until next time, keep solving problems, keep playing, and keep planning!

Alex & Jordan <3

Extra Challenge

This extra challenge is a little bit more complex than the main challenges in the book and represents some of the longer answer questions where you might be asked to combine your knowledge of different programming techniques and data structures to solve a more in-depth problem.

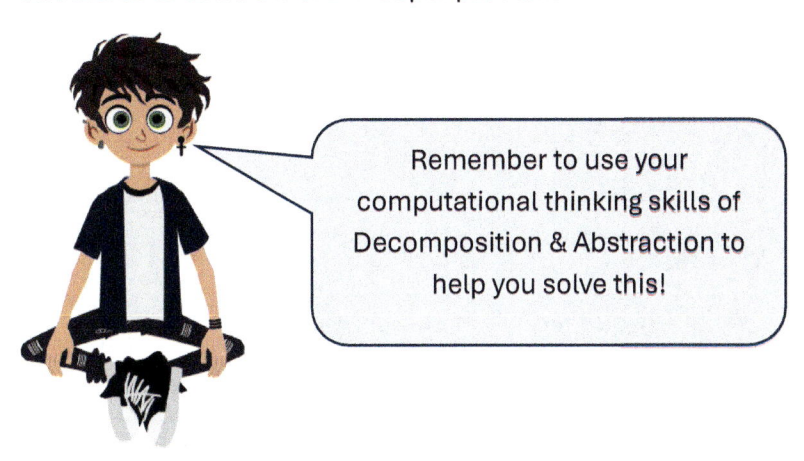

> Remember to use your computational thinking skills of Decomposition & Abstraction to help you solve this!

The Digital Invitation Challenge

For the next games night, Jordan decides to use a digital invitation that gathers RSVPs and taps into their friends' gaming preferences. This will help the friends to plan the games for the evening in advance.

Jordan needs your help to design a program that captures each friend's name, age, and favourite game from a list. The program must include checks to ensure all entered data is valid and then count up the game preferences to identify the top three games for the event.

The array gameOptions already exists with the data below and you do not need to declare or populate this this in your code.

Game	Tally
Chess	5
Monopoly	3
Scrabble	4
Catan	2
Risk	1
Ticket to Ride	2
Carcassonne	0
Pandemic	2

Your Task:

Create a pseudocode program that will:

- Collect user **input** of Name, age, and favourite game.
- **Validates the input data by** ensuring the name is present, the age is within a reasonable range (11 to 17 inclusive), and the name is not blank.
    a. If the age is out of range or the name is blank, the program should **output** a suitable error message.
    b. If a guest inputs a game that **doesn't exist** in the gameOptions array, the program should **output** the options again.
- **Increment** the tally for each game that a guest selects as their favourite.

Alex & Jordan Design an Adventure

- **Append** each friend's details to a new **2D array** called `guestList`.

- Use the data entered to **output** the most popular three games in a user friendly format. For example:
  ```
  "Choice 1: Monopoly
   Choice 2 : Risk
   Choice 3: Chess"
  ```

Help with Decomposition

This challenge doesn't need to be solved as one big block of code. Instead, try breaking it down into five main steps that you use to build a bigger program.

Step 1: Data Inputs
Step 2: Validation
Step 3: Update Guest List
Step 4: Update Favourite Game Tally
Step 5: Identify Top Three Games

Even if you don't solve all five steps completely the first time, solving just a few of the steps with good coding practices and comments will help move you towards a final solution.

Answers

The answers shown here aren't the only solution for a pseudocode question. Programs can be solved in many different ways, but these answers and explanations will show you an example solution in a style that an examiner will be familiar with.

When writing pseudocode, the most important things to remember are that you should clearly show your logic and be consistent with your style.

There are a few useful tips that help when writing algorithms in pseudocode:

- ☑ **Use meaningful identifiers** – your variable and data structure names should be named so that other people understand what they're for

- ☑ **Indent your code** – the computer doesn't care about whitespace, but humans do! If you bunch your code up without spaces and indentation it makes it difficult to read.

- ☑ **Add comments** – if you're answering a particular question, add a //comment to explain how your code meets the question criteria.

- ☑ **Don't panic!** – Allow yourself some time to think about the logic before you start writing. It's ok to write a quick plan first for longer questions.

Problem 1 – Input & Output

Example Solution:

```
DECLARE friendName : STRING
DECLARE favouriteGame : STRING

OUTPUT "Enter your friend's name: "
INPUT friendName
OUTPUT "Enter your friend's favorite board game: "
INPUT favouriteGame

OUTPUT "You've added " + friendName + " who loves playing " + favouriteGame + "."
```

Step-by-Step Explanation:

Step 1: Declaring Variables:

At the top of the pseudocode, any variables used in the program are stated with their data type.

A variable called `friendName` is created that will be used to store a string value for the name of each person.

Then another variable named `favouriteGame` is created to store the name of the friend's favourite board game, which is also a string.

Step 2: Getting the Name:

A message is output to the screen asking the user to enter their friend's name. This is also called a prompt.

The INPUT will cause the program to pause until the user types into the screen and presses Enter.

The data that the user types in is then stored in the `friendName` variable.

Step 3: Getting Their Favourite Game:

Another output is sent to the screen, but this time it's asking for the name of the friend's favourite board game.

The INPUT will wait for the user to type the name of the board game and stores that value in the `favouriteGame` variable.

Step 4: Outputting A Concatenated Message:

Finally, the last line outputs a confirmation message that combines the text "You've added " with the `friendName` variable and the `favouriteGame` variable to let the user know that the information has been successfully recorded.

Concatenation

The + symbol is used to concatenate (*join together*), the string of text with the variables `friendName` and `favouriteGame`.

Problem 2 – Input & Output (Player Data)

Example Solution:

```
DECLARE friendName : STRING
DECLARE numberOfGames : INTEGER
DECLARE gamePreference : STRING

OUTPUT "Enter your friend's name: "
INPUT friendName
OUTPUT "How many games does " + friendName + " want to play? "
INPUT numberOfGames
OUTPUT "Does " + friendName + " prefer strategy or chance games? (Enter 'strategy' or 'chance') "
INPUT gamePreference

OUTPUT friendName + " wants to play " + numberOfGames + " games and prefers " + gamePreference + " games."
```

Step-by-Step Explanation:

Step 1: Declaring Variables:

At the top of the pseudocode, any variables used in the program are stated with their data type.

Step 2: Inputting Friend's Name:

First, we prompt Alex and Jordan to enter their friend's name, then capture and store that name in the variable `friendName` for later use.

Step 3: Inputting the Number of Games:

Next, we ask how many games the friend wishes to play. This numerical input is stored in the variable `numberOfGames`.

Step 4: Input Game Preference:

Understanding whether the friend prefers strategy games or chance games will help Alex and Jordan select the right games for the night. The user inputs this preference, which is stored in the variable `gamePreference`.

Step 5: Outputting Preferences:

Finally, we add an output a message that outputs a meaningful message. This concatenates (joins together) the `friendName`, the `numberOfGames`, and `gamePreference` variables to create a sentence.

Problem 3 – IF, THEN, ELSE

Example Solution:

```
DECLARE numberOfPlayers : INTEGER

OUTPUT "How many players will be playing?"
INPUT numberOfPlayers

IF numberOfPlayers >= 4 THEN
    OUTPUT "We recommend playing 'Galactic
Defenders' for your group size!"
ELSE
    OUTPUT "For a smaller group, 'Mystery
Mansion' is perfect."
ENDIF
```

Step-by-Step Explanation:

Step 1: Declaring Variables:

At the top of the pseudocode, any variables used in the program are stated with their data type.

Step 2: Inputting the Number of Players:

We then prompt the user with "How many players will be playing?" and use the INPUT statement to capture the user's response, storing it in `numberOfPlayers`.

Step 3: Using IF and ELSE for Selection & Output:

The IF statement checks if `numberOfPlayers` is greater than or equal to 4. This condition is used to decide which game to recommend based on the group size.

If the condition (`numberOfPlayers >= 4`) is true, it means the group is large enough for "Castle Panic". Therefore, the program outputs a recommendation for "Galactic Defenders".

If the condition is false (meaning the number of players is less than 4), the ELSE part of the structure is executed. In this case, "Mystery Mansion" is suggested.

Problem 4 – Choosing A Game

Example Solution:

```
DECLARE numberOfPlayers : INTEGER

OUTPUT "How many players will be attending the game night?"
INPUT numberOfPlayers

IF numberOfPlayers = 2 THEN
    OUTPUT "For 2 players, we recommend 'Puzzle Quest'. Enjoy the challenge!"
ELSE IF numberOfPlayers = 3 THEN
    OUTPUT "With 3 players, 'Mystery Mansion' is a fantastic choice. Have fun exploring!"
ELSE IF numberOfPlayers = 4 THEN
    OUTPUT "For 4 players, 'Galactic Defenders' is perfect for a team adventure!"
ELSE
    OUTPUT "For more than 4 players, 'Empire Builders' will make your game night epic!"
ENDIF
```

Step-by-Step Explanation:

Step 1: Declaring Variables:

At the top of the pseudocode, any variables used in the program are stated with their data type.

Step 2: Inputting the Number of Players:

The first step in the logic involves asking the participants of the game night how many players will be attending. This question sets the stage for the selection process by storing the inputted number in a variable named `numberOfPlayers`.

Step 2: Using Selection:

The initial IF statement checks if `numberOfPlayers` equals 2. If this condition is true, it recommends "Puzzle Quest".

The ELSE IF statements check for 3 and 4 players in sequence, recommending "Mystery Mansion" and "Galactic Defenders" based on the group's size.

The final ELSE statement is used for any situation where the number of players exceeds 4, recommending "Empire Builders".

Step 3: Outputting the Recommendation:

Based on the number of players, the pseudocode outputs the most suitable game recommendation in each IF statement.

Problem 5 – CASE of Snacks!

Example Solution:

```
DECLARE gameChosen : STRING

OUTPUT "Which game have you chosen for game night? Please enter: "
INPUT gameChosen

CASE gameChosen OF
    "Puzzle Quest": OUTPUT "Popcorn is the perfect snack for 'Puzzle Quest'!"
    "Mystery Mansion": OUTPUT "Chocolate Chip Cookies will make 'Mystery Mansion' even more enjoyable!"
    "Galactic Defenders": OUTPUT "Why not have some Pizza while saving the galaxy in 'Galactic Defenders'?"
    "Empire Builders": OUTPUT "Pretzels are great for building empires in 'Empire Builders'!"
    OTHERWISE: OUTPUT "Any snack is good, but choosing a game first might be better!"
ENDCASE
```

Step-by-Step Explanation:

Step 1: Declaring Variables:

At the top of the pseudocode, any variables used in the program are stated with their data type.

Step 2: Choosing the Game:

The user is prompted to enter the name of their chosen game which is stored in the variable gameChosen, for use in the CASE statement decision.

Step 3: Selecting the Snack:

A CASE statement is used to match the user's input (the chosen game) with a corresponding snack recommendation.

Each game title is a "case" that, when matched, triggers an output recommending a specific snack.

An OTHERWISE case is included to handle any inputs that don't match the known game titles, similar to the ELSE in the IF,ELSE statements.

Step 4: Outputting the Snack Recommendation:

Depending on the user's game choice, the program outputs the corresponding snack recommendation indented inside its CASE.

Problem 6 – Seating Plan List

Example Solution:

```
DECLARE seating : ARRAY[0..5] of STRING
seating[0] ← "Alex"
seating[1] ← "Jordan"
seating[2] ← "Taylor"
seating[3] ← "Morgan"
seating[4] ← "Casey"
seating[5] ← "Jamie"

FOR i ← 0 TO 5 DO
    OUTPUT "Seat " + (i+1) + ": " + seating[i]
NEXT i
```

Step-by-Step Explanation:

Step 1: Setting Up the Seating Array:

The algorithm begins with the declaration of a 1D array named seating, which is allocated six slots. Each slot corresponds to a seat at the table and is filled with the names of Alex, Jordan, and their four friends: Taylor, Morgan, Casey, and Jamie.

Step 2: Using a FOR Loop to Iterate Through the Array:

To output the seating plan, a FOR loop is used as we know how many times to loop. This loop iterates over each index of the seating array, starting from 0 (Alex) and ending at 5 (Jamie).

Step 3: Outputting Each Seat and Corresponding Name:

Inside the loop, a message is output for each seat by combining the current index i (*with 1 added to it for user-friendly seat numbering*) and the name stored at that index in the seating array.

Why the Keyword *NEXT i* is used at the end of a FOR loop:

The keyword NEXT i signifies the end of the loop's block of instructions and instructs the program to return to the top of the FOR statement. Using NEXT i shows that the count controller variable i is incremented (*1 is added*), moving the process to the next index of the array.

Problem 7 – The Dice Roll Shuffle

Example Solution:

```
DECLARE seating : ARRAY[0..5] of STRING
DECLARE diceRoll, newSeat : INTEGER
seating[0] ← "Alex"
seating[1] ← "Jordan"
seating[2] ← "Taylor"
seating[3] ← "Morgan"
seating[4] ← "Casey"
seating[5] ← "Jamie"

diceRoll ← ROUND(RANDOM() * 6, 0)

FOR i ← 0 TO 5 DO
    newSeat ← (i + diceRoll) MOD 6
    OUTPUT "Seat " + (i+1) + " moves to Seat " + (newSeat+1) + ": " + seating[i] + " -> " + seating[newSeat]
NEXT i
```

Step-by-Step Explanation:

Step 1: Setting Up the Seating and Simulating a Dice Roll:

The algorithm starts by declaring an array called `seating` to store the names of all players. Just like before, this helps us organize who is sitting where.

The `diceRoll` variable is used to simulate rolling a 6-sided dice. Because `RANDOM` creates a number between 0 & 1, this is multiplied by 6 to get a number between 1 & 6, although this will be a decimal number. `ROUND` is used to change this into an integer.

Step 2: Calculating New Seats:

The algorithm uses a `FOR` loop to go through each seat, from Alex in seat 0 to Jamie in seat 5.

For each player, we calculate their new seat after moving clockwise. The formula `(i + diceRoll) MOD 6` finds the new seat number. We use `MOD 6` because there are 6 seats – the `MOD` function finds the remainder after division, and this ensures that if the calculation exceeds 5 (the last seat), it loops back to the beginning.

Step 3: Outputting the New Seating Arrangement:

Inside the loop, the algorithm outputs a message that tells us where each player moves. It shows the original seat, the new seat, and who is moving. This helps everyone understand the new seating arrangement before the next game starts.

Why `MOD 6` is Important:

The `MOD` operation is a mathematical way of finding the remainder after division. In this example, it makes sure that seat numbers wrap around correctly. If a player is supposed to move beyond seat 5, `MOD 6` loops their position back to the start of the array, mimicking a round table.

Problem 8 – Voting for Games

Example Solution:

```
DECLARE games : ARRAY[0..3] of STRING
DECLARE votes : ARRAY[0..3] of INTEGER
DECLARE maxVotes, winnerIndex : INTEGER
games[0] ← "Puzzle Quest"
games[1] ← "Mystery Mansion"
games[2] ← "Galactic Defenders"
games[3] ← "Empire Builders"
votes[0] ← 0
votes[1] ← 0
votes[2] ← 0
votes[3] ← 0

// Simulate voting
votes[0] ← 2 // Two votes for Puzzle Quest
votes[1] ← 1 // One vote for Mystery Mansion
votes[2] ← 3 // Three votes for Galactic
Defenders
votes[3] ← 0 // No votes for Empire Builders

// Find the game with the most votes
maxVotes ← votes[0]
winnerIndex ← 0
FOR i ← 1 TO 3 DO
    IF votes[i] > maxVotes THEN
        maxVotes ← votes[i]
        winnerIndex ← i
    ENDIF
NEXT i

OUTPUT "The next game to play is: " +
games[winnerIndex] + " with " + maxVotes + "
votes."
```

Step-by-Step Explanation:

Step 1: Setting Up the Arrays:

First, the algorithm creates two parallel arrays: `games` holds the names of the games available for voting, and `votes` tracks how many votes each game receives. Initially, all games have 0 votes.

Step 2: Simulating Voting:

To keep the example simple, we've simulated the voting process by directly assigning vote counts to each game in the votes array. You may want to make this more realistic by using input statements.

Step 3: Tallying Votes and Finding the Winner:

To identify which game has the most votes, we start by assuming the first game has the maximum votes. We then use a FOR loop to compare this with the votes for the other games.

If we find a game with more votes than our current maximum, we update `maxVotes` with this new number and `winnerIndex` with the index of this game. The `winnerIndex` helps us keep track of which game is currently winning.

After going through all the games, `winnerIndex` will point to the game with the most votes, and `maxVotes` will tell us how many votes it received.

Step 4: Outputting the Winning Game:

Finally, we output the name of the game with the most votes and how many votes it got. This tells everyone which game will be played next.

Problem 9 – The Scoreboard

Example Solution:

```
DECLARE scores : ARRAY[0..5][0..3] of INTEGER
DECLARE playerTotalScores : ARRAY[0..5] of
INTEGER
DECLARE i, j, total : INTEGER

// Saving the scores in a 2D array
scores[0][0] ← 5 // Alex, Game 1
scores[0][1] ← 8 // Alex, Game 2
scores[0][2] ← 7 // Alex, Game 3
scores[0][3] ← 6 // Alex, Game 4

scores[1][0] ← 3 // Jordan, Game 1
scores[1][1] ← 5 // Jordan, Game 2
//... continue assigning scores for all players

// Initialize total scores to 0
FOR i ← 0 TO 5 DO
    playerTotalScores[i] ← 0
NEXT i

// Calculate total scores for each player
FOR i ← 0 TO 5 DO
    total ← 0
    FOR j ← 0 TO 3 DO
        total ← total + scores[i][j]
    NEXT j
    playerTotalScores[i] ← total
    OUTPUT "Total score for Player " + (i+1) + ":
" + total
NEXT i
```

Step-by-Step Explanation:

Step 1: Storing Scores in a 2D Array:

A 2D array named `scores` is created to store the individual game scores for each player. The first dimension (rows) represents each player, and the second dimension (columns) represents each game. The scores are assigned using two indexes for the row and column.

Step 2: Initializing Total Scores Array:

Another array named `playerTotalScores` is declared & initialized to keep track of the total scores for each player. A FOR loop sets each player's total score to 0 to start with a clean slate.

Step 3: Calculating and Outputting Total Scores:

Finally, the algorithm calculates the total scores using nested FOR loops. The outer loop goes through each player, while the inner loop sums the scores for all four games.

The variable called `total` is used to keep a running total of the scores for each player. After all the games are added up, the total score is assigned to the corresponding item in `playerTotalScores`.

An OUTPUT statement shows the total score for each player after all of the calculations are finished.

Problem 10 – Player Badges

Example Solution:

```
DECLARE Scoreboard : ARRAY[0..5][0..3] of INTEGER
DECLARE badges : ARRAY[0..5] of STRING
DECLARE playerNames : ARRAY[0..5] of STRING
DECLARE playerTotalScores : ARRAY[0..5] of
INTEGER
DECLARE total : INTEGER

// Names of the players
playerNames[0] ← "Alex"
playerNames[1] ← "Jordan"
playerNames[2] ← "Taylor"
playerNames[3] ← "Morgan"
playerNames[4] ← "Casey"
playerNames[5] ← "Jamie"

// Initialize total scores and badges
FOR i ← 0 TO 5 DO
    total ← 0
    FOR j ← 0 TO 3 DO
        total ← total + Scoreboard[i][j]
    NEXT j
    playerTotalScores[i] ← total
    // Assign badges based on the total score
    IF total = 40 THEN
        badges[i] ← "Perfectionist"
    ELSE IF total > 20 THEN
        badges[i] ← "Strategist"
    ELSE IF total > 10 THEN
        badges[i] ← "Optimist"
    ELSE
        badges[i] ← "Newbie"
    ENDIF
NEXT i
```

```
// Output each player's name, total score, and 
badge
FOR i ← 0 TO 5 DO
    OUTPUT "Player: " + playerNames[i] + ", Total 
Score: " + playerTotalScores[i] + ", Badge: " + 
badges[i]
NEXT i
```

Step-by-Step Explanation:

Step 1: Declare Variables & Data Structures (arrays)

The arrays for badges, playerNames, and PlayerTotalScores have been declared to save the data related to each player. The variable total is also declared to calculate each player's total score from the leaderboard.

Step 2: Sum the Scores for Each Player

The algorithm uses a FOR loop to iterate over each of the 6 players by using i ← 0 TO 5.

Inside the first FOR loop, the variable total is assigned the value 0. This means that it will reset for each player.

Within this loop, sum up the scores from the Scoreboard array for all four games.

Step 3: Identify the Right Badge for Each Player

Still within the loop for each player, the algorithm uses a series of IF and ELSE IF statements to assign the badge based on the total score.

It then stores the badge in the badges array at the same index as the name of the player and their row of scores.

Step 4: Output Each Player's Information

Finally, the algorithm uses another FOR loop to iterate over each player again.

This time, it outputs the player's name, their total score, and their assigned badge as a concatenated sentence.

Problem 11 – Mini Maths Challenge

Example Solution:

```
DECLARE diceRoll1, diceRoll2, finalScore,
operationIndex : INTEGER
DECLARE operation : STRING
DECLARE operations : ARRAY[1..6] of STRING

operations[1] ← "+"
operations[2] ← "-"
operations[3] ← "*"
operations[4] ← "/"
operations[5] ← "DIV"
operations[6] ← "MOD"

// Simulate rolling two 6-sided dice
diceRoll1 ← ROUND(RANDOM() * 6, 0)
diceRoll2 ← ROUND(RANDOM() * 6, 0)

// Simulate spinning the spinner to choose an operation
operationIndex ← ROUND(RANDOM() * 6, 0)
operation ← operations[operationIndex]

// Perform the operation
IF operation = "+" THEN
    finalScore ← diceRoll1 + diceRoll2
ELSE IF operation = "-" THEN
    finalScore ← diceRoll1 - diceRoll2
ELSE IF operation = "*" THEN
    finalScore ← diceRoll1 * diceRoll2
ELSE IF operation = "/" THEN
    finalScore ← diceRoll1 / diceRoll2
```

```
ELSE IF operation = "DIV" THEN
    finalScore ← diceRoll1 DIV diceRoll2
ELSE IF operation = "MOD" THEN
    finalScore ← diceRoll1 MOD diceRoll2
ENDIF

// Output the results
OUTPUT "First roll: " + diceRoll1
OUTPUT "Operation: " + operation
OUTPUT "Second roll: " + diceRoll2
OUTPUT "Final score: " + finalScore
```

Step-by-Step Explanation:

Step 1: Storing Scores in a 2D Array:

The algorithm starts by declaring all of the variables and data structures (arrays) that will be used in the program.

An array called `operations` is included in this and is used to store the possible mathematical operations that can be performed in the game. This simulates the spinner.

Step 2: Simulate Dice Rolls and Spinner

The algorithm then uses the ROUND and RANDOM functions to generate two numbers to simulate dice rolls (`diceRoll1` and `diceRoll2`).

Another random number is created to select an operation from the operations array to simulate spinning the spinner.

Step 3: Calculate the Final Score

Using IF and ELSE IF statements, the algorithm determines which mathematical operation to apply based on the result of the spinner. (*this could be more efficient if a CASE statement was used & is shown in the next solution*)

The chosen operation is performed on the two dice rolls and assigned to the variable called `finalScore`.

Step 4: Output the Game Result

Finally, the results are output to show the player's first roll, the chosen operation, the second roll, and the final score after applying the maths.

Problem 12 – Maths Challenge Function

Example Solution:

```
DECLARE diceRoll1, diceRoll2 : INTEGER

PROCEDURE PerformMathChallenge(dice1: INTEGER,
dice2: INTEGER)
  DECLARE choice, finalScore : INTEGER
  DECLARE operation : STRING

  // Simulate spinning the spinner to choose an
  operation
  choice ← ROUND(RANDOM() * 6, 0)
  CASE choice OF
    1:  operation ← "+"
        finalScore ← dice1 + dice2

    2:  operation ← "-"
        finalScore ← dice1 - dice2

    3:  operation ← "*"
        finalScore ← dice1 * dice2

    4:  operation ← "/"
        // Check to prevent division by zero
        IF dice2 = 0 THEN
            finalScore ← 0
        ELSE
            finalScore ← dice1 / dice2
        ENDIF
```

```
    5:  operation ← "DIV"
        // Check to prevent division by zero
        IF dice2 = 0 THEN
            finalScore ← 0
        ELSE
            finalScore ← dice1 DIV dice2
        ENDIF
    6:
        operation ← "MOD"
        // Check to prevent division by zero
        IF dice2 = 0 THEN
            finalScore ← dice1
        ELSE
            finalScore ← dice1 MOD dice2
        ENDIF
  ENDCASE
  // Output the results
  OUTPUT "First roll: " + dice1
  OUTPUT "Operation: " + operation
  OUTPUT "Second roll: " + dice2
  OUTPUT "Final score: " + finalScore
ENDPROCEDURE

// Simulate rolling two 6-sided dice
diceRoll1 ← ROUND(RANDOM() * 6, 0)
diceRoll2 ← ROUND(RANDOM() * 6, 0)

CALL PerformMathChallenge(diceRoll1, diceRoll2)
```

Step-by-Step Explanation:

The answer shown here includes some extra error checking to prevent the program from crashing. As it's mathematically impossible to divide by zero, if this does happen, the algorithm will set a default value of dice1.

Step 1: Storing Scores in a 2D Array:

The algorithm declares the two dice variable for the main program: `diceRoll1` & `diceRoll2`

Step 2: Declaring the Procedure

The procedure called `PerformMathChallenge` that will perform the logic of the game is created with two parameters to match the dice rolls called `dice1` & `dice2`

Step 3: Storing Scores in a 2D Array:

The algorithm declares and initializes the variables that are used inside the procedure (local variables) which are: `choice`, and `finalScore`.

Step 4: Simulate the Spinner

A CASE statement is used to select the operation saved in the variable `choice`, representing the spin of a spinner.

Step 5: Calculate the Final Score

Inside the CASE statement, the algorithm matches the value of the variable `choice` to a case corresponding to one of the six operations. Depending on the case, it assigns the operation and calculates `finalScore`.

For division operations, there are checks to prevent division by zero. If `diceRoll2` is 0, it sets `finalScore` to a default value of `diceRoll1`.

Step 5: Output the Game Result

The algorithm outputs the results, showing the first dice roll, the operation performed, the second dice roll, and the final score after the operation.

Step 6: Generate Dice Throws

Outside of the procedure, two random numbers are generated using the ROUND and RANDOM functions, simulating the roll of two 6-sided dice.

Step 7: Call the Procedure

The procedure `PerformMathChallenge` is called and the two dice throws are included in the brackets as data to pass into the subroutine.

Why Use A CASE Statement?

The use of a CASE statement here allows for a more efficient way of associating each spinner outcome with a specific operation. When a selection statement uses more than 2 `ELSE IF` statements, it's worth considering using a CASE instead.

Problem 13 – Jamie's Secret Code

Example Solution:

```
DECLARE playerNum1, playerNum2, code : INTEGER

FUNCTION GenerateSecretCode(num1: INTEGER, num2:
INTEGER) RETURNS INTEGER
    DECLARE secretCode : INTEGER
    secretCode ← (num1 * 3 + num2) / 2
    RETURN secretCode
ENDFUNCTION

// Main Program

OUTPUT "Enter the first number:"
INPUT playerNum1
OUTPUT "Enter the second number:"
INPUT playerNum2

code ← GenerateSecretCode(playerNum1, playerNum2)
OUTPUT "The secret code is: " + code
```

Step-by-Step Explanation:

Step 1: Declare Main Program Variables:

Three integer variables are declared. `playerNum1`, `playerNum2` are created to store the player inputs and `code` is created to store the value returned by the function.

Step 2: Define the Function

The algorithm defines a function called GenerateSecretCode that takes two integers as parameters. This function runs the logic for generating the secret code and will return an integer when its complete.

Step 3: Perform Calculations Inside the Function

Within the function, the algorithm declares a variable called secretCode.

The secret code is calculated by tripling the first number (num1 * 3), adding the second number (+ num2), and then dividing the result by 2.

The calculated value is stored in the secretCode variable.

Step 4: Return the Secret Code

The function completes its task by returning the value of the variable secretCode.

The RETURN keyword is used to tell the function to send this value back to the part of the program that called it.

Step 5: Obtain User Input and Call the Function

Outside the function, the players are prompted to enter two numbers that are stored in the variables playerNum1 and playerNum2.

The GenerateSecretCode function is called with the player's numbers as the parameters. It's returned value is stored in the variable called code.

Step 6: Output the Result

Finally, output the secret code to the players, revealing the number they need to continue their quest for the Golden Token.

Problem 14 – The Puzzle Piece Shuffle

Example Solution:

```
DECLARE puzzlePieces : ARRAY OF INTEGER
DECLARE shuffledPieces : ARRAY OF INTEGER
DECLARE n : INTEGER

FUNCTION ShuffleArray(pieces: ARRAY OF INTEGER)
RETURNS ARRAY OF INTEGER
    DECLARE i, j, temp : INTEGER
    FOR i ← 0 TO LEN(pieces) - 1 DO
        j ← ROUND(RANDOM() * LEN(pieces) - 1, 0)
        temp ← pieces[i] //swap
        pieces[i] ← pieces[j]
        pieces[j] ← temp
    NEXT i
    RETURN pieces
ENDFUNCTION

// Main Program

OUTPUT "Enter the number of puzzle pieces:"
INPUT n
FOR i ← 0 TO n - 1 DO
    puzzlePieces[i] ← i + 1
NEXT i

shuffledPieces ← ShuffleArray(puzzlePieces)

OUTPUT "Here are your shuffled puzzle pieces:"
FOR i ← 0 TO LEN(shuffledPieces) - 1 DO
    OUTPUT shuffledPieces[i]
NEXT i
```

Step-by-Step Explanation:

Step 1: Declare Main Program Variables:

Two arrays of integers are declared called `puzzlePieces` to store the original puzzle, and `shuffledPieces` to store the shuffled version shown to the player.

The algorithm also declares a variable called n are created to store the inputs of the number of puzzle pieces.

Step 2: Define the Shuffle Function

The algorithm defines a function called `ShuffleArray` that takes an array of integers (pieces) as input and rearranges the array's items into random order.

Step 3: Implement the Shuffling Algorithm

Inside the function, the algorithm uses a FOR loop to iterate over each item the array up to the penultimate (second to last) item.

In each loop, a random index called j is generated, then the item at the current index (i) is swapped with the item at index j. As only one item can be moved at a time, a temporary variable called temp is used to hold the current item to prevent it from being overwritten.

Step 4: Return the Shuffled Array

Once the array has been shuffled, the RETURN keyword is used to send the shuffled array back to where the function was called.

Step 5: Create the Puzzle Pieces Array

Outside the function, the player for the number of puzzle pieces and create an array called `puzzlePieces` with items from 1 to n, representing the puzzle pieces.

Step 6: Call the Shuffle Function and Output the Result

Finally, the `ShuffleArray` function is called, using the `puzzlePieces` array as a parameter and the returned result is stored in yje variable called `shuffledPieces`.

The algorithm then iterates through the `shuffledPieces` array with a FOR loop and outputs each shuffled puzzle piece so the player knows their starting set.

Problem 15 – Puzzling Linear Search

Example Solution:

```
DECLARE puzzlePieces : ARRAY OF INTEGER
DECLARE pieceToFind, pos : INTEGER
DECLARE found : BOOLEAN

// Example array of puzzle pieces
puzzlePieces ← [5, 3, 7, 1, 9, 2, 8, 4, 6]

// Main Program
OUTPUT "Enter the puzzle piece number to find:"
INPUT pieceToFind

found ← FALSE
pos ← 0

WHILE found = FALSE AND pos < LEN(puzzlePieces)
    IF puzzlePieces[pos] = pieceToFind THEN
        found ← TRUE
    ELSE
        pos ← pos + 1
    ENDIF
END WHILE

IF found = TRUE THEN
    OUTPUT "Piece found at position: " + pos
ELSE
    OUTPUT "Piece not found."
ENDIF
```

Step-by-Step Explanation:

Step 1: Declare Variables & Data Structures:

The algorithm starts by declaring an array called `puzzlePieces` which is used to hold the puzzle pieces.

After this, `pieceToFind` is is ceated as an integer variable for the user to input the number of the puzzle piece they're searching for.

The variable called `pos` (*short for position*) keeps track of the current index being checked in the array. `found` is a boolean variable indicating whether the piece has been found.

Step 2: Initialize the Puzzle Pieces Array:

The array `puzzlePieces` is assigned initial values with example data so that the program runs.

Step 3: User Input for Puzzle Piece to Find:

The algorithm prompts the user to enter the number of the puzzle piece they wish to find. This is stored in the variable called `pieceToFind`.

Step 4: Prepare for Search:

The variables `found` and `pos` are initialized. `found` is set to FALSE to indicate the piece hasn't been found yet, and `pos` is set to 0, the starting index of the array.

Step 5: Perform A Linear Search:

The algorithm uses a WHILE loop which repeats as long as two conditions are met: the piece has not been found (`found = FALSE`) and the current position is less than the length of the puzzlePieces array (`pos < LEN(puzzlePieces)`).

Inside the loop, an IF statement checks if the current puzzle piece (`puzzlePieces[pos]`) matches the value of `pieceToFind`.

If a match is found, `found` is set to TRUE, indicating the search is successful and the WHILE loop will stop.

If no match is found, the `pos` variable is incremented by 1, moving the search to the next position in the array.

Step 6: Output the Search Result:

After the loop, another `IF` statement checks the value of the variable `found`.

If `found = TRUE`, this indicates that the piece was found, so the program outputs the position where the piece was found. Since pos starts at 0, you could consider adding 1 to pos when displaying the position to the user to make this easier for them to understand (*as we usually count from 1 instead of 0*).

If the piece was not found (`found = FALSE`), the program outputs "Piece not found."

Problem 16 – Bubble Sort Tokens

Example Solution:

```
DECLARE tokens : ARRAY OF INTEGER
DECLARE temp : INTEGER
DECLARE sorted : BOOLEAN

tokens ← [5, 3, 7, 1, 9, 2, 8, 4, 6]

sorted ← FALSE
WHILE sorted = FALSE
    sorted ← TRUE
    FOR i ← 0 TO LEN(tokens) - 2 DO
        IF tokens[i] > tokens[i + 1] THEN
            temp ← tokens[i]
            tokens[i] ← tokens[i + 1]
            tokens[i + 1] ← temp
            sorted ← FALSE
        ENDIF
    NEXT i
END WHILE

OUTPUT "Sorted tokens: "
FOR i ← 0 TO LEN(tokens) - 1 DO
    OUTPUT tokens[i]
NEXT i
```

Step-by-Step Explanation:

Step 1: Declare the Array and Variables

The algorithm starts by declaring an array called `tokens` to hold the jumbled numbers. After this, variables for a temporary holder for swapping (`temp`), and a flag (`sorted`) are declared.

Step 2: Initialize the Sorting Process

The `sorted` flag variable is initially set to FALSE to start the sorting process. This allows the while loop to start, and the flag will be used in the loop to determine when the sorting is complete.

Step 3: Implement Bubble Sort

A WHILE loop is used to repeat as long as the variable `sorted` equals FALSE.

At the beginning of each repetition of the WHILE loop, `sorted` is set to TRUE as we assume that the list is sorted until we encounter a pair of numbers that need to be swapped.

Inside the `WHILE` loop, a FOR loop is used to iterate over the array, comparing items in pairs. If an item is found to be greater than the next, they are swapped, and `sorted` is set back to FALSE, indicating that another pass is necessary.

This process repeats until no swaps are needed, at which point sorted remains TRUE, and the `WHILE` loop ends.

Step 4: Output the Sorted Array

Finally, another FOR loop iterates through the sorted tokens array, outputting each token in the new, sorted order.

Problem 17 – Hidden Strings

Example Solution:

The solution below shows how this algorithm would be implemented for the first clue. This would be repeated for each clue.

```
DECLARE note1, finalClue1: STRING
DECLARE clues1 : ARRAY[0..8][0..2] of INTEGER

note1 ← "X7bQTheX5firstX2clueX9isX4nearX8theX6oldX3oakX1tree."

clues1 ← [[5,3], [10,5], [17,4], [23,2], [27,4], [33,3], [38,3], [43,3], [48,4]]

finalClue1 ← ""
FOR i ← 0 TO LENGTH(clues1) DO
    finalClue1 ← finalClue1 + SUBSTRING(note1,
                 clues1[i][0], clues1[i][1])
NEXT i

OUTPUT "The first clue is: " + finalClue1
```

Step-by-Step Explanation:

Step 1: Declare Variables and Arrays

The algorithm starts by declaring the variables to use in the program. The variable `note1` is a string that stores the first secret note.

`finalClue1` is a string variable that will hold the concatenated clue extracted from `note1`.

`clues1` is a 2D array of integers, where each row holds two numbers: the start position and the length of a substring to be extracted from `note1`.

Step 2: Initialize the Secret Note and Clues Array

The algorithm assigns `note1` the string given to us in the problem which contains the clue.

The array `clues1` is filled with the start positions and lengths for each part of the clue within `note1`. *For notes 2 & 3, you'll need to calculate these.*

Step 3: Extract and Concatenate the Clues

A FOR loop is used to iterate over the clues1 array. For each loop, it uses the SUBSTRING function to extract a part of the clue based on the start position and length specified in the current row of `clues1`.

The algorithm then appends the substring to `finalClue1` to create a new string out of the extracted substrings.

Step 4: Output the Final Clue

After the loop completes, `finalClue1` contains the full clue, constructed by concatenating all the extracted substrings. The algorithm outputs this clue.

Problem 18 – The ASCII Padlock

Example Solution:

```
DECLARE word, padlockCombination : STRING
DECLARE i, asciiValue : INTEGER

FUNCTION single_digit(num)
   digits ← STRING(num)
   WHILE LENGTH(digits) > 1
      n ← 0
      FOR i ← 0 TO LENGTH(digits)-1
         n ← n + INT(SUBSTRING(digits,i,1))
      NEXT i
   END WHILE
   RETURN STRING(n)

OUTPUT "Enter the secret word:"
INPUT word

padlockCombination ← ""

FOR i ← 1 TO LENGTH(word)
   IF i MOD 2 = 0 THEN
      asciiValue ← ORD(UCASE(SUBSTRING(word,i,1)))
   ELSE
      asciiValue ← ORD(LCASE(SUBSTRING(word,i,1)))
   ENDIF

   padlockCombination ← padlockCombination +
                        single_digit(asciiValue)
NEXT i

OUTPUT "Padlock Combination: " +
padlockCombination
```

Step-by-Step Explanation:

Step 1: Declare Variables and Arrays

Two string variables are declared at the start of the algorithm. The variable called word stores the user's input of the word they are testing with the padlock. The `padlockCombination` variable holds the string of numbers created from the input word.

Step 2: Get The User's Input

The program starts by asking the user to input a secret word. This word will be transformed into the padlock combination.

Step 3: Initialize Variables

The variable `padlockCombination` is initialized as an empty string. It needs to hold this empty string to allow the algorithm to concatenate on the end of it. An empty string still counts as a value.

Step 3: Check if the Position is Odd or Even

The algorithm uses a FOR loop to iterate over each character in the input word.

The program then checks if the value of the count controller variable i is even or odd:

If it's even (`i MOD 2 = 0`), the character is converted to uppercase using UCASE.

If odd, the character is converted to lowercase using LCASE.

Step 4: Convert Each Letter to ASCII

Inside the IF statements, the current letter is extracted using SUBSTRING with I as the position to get the letter from, then converted to its ASCII number using the ORD function:

`ORD(UCASE(SUBSTRING(word,i,1)))`

Step 5: Create A Single Digit

Once the ASCII number has been calculated, it is appended to the end of the variable padlockCombination. Before appending happens, the single_digit function is called which converts the number into a single digit by:

Taking the ASCII number and turning it into a string called digits. Then, a WHILE will repeat until the length of digits is 1.

Inside the WHILE loop, a variable called n is given the value of zero. Then a FOR loop converts each character of digits into a number and adds this to the value of n (this is called a totaller).

As a WHILE loop has been used, if the result is still more than one digit, this will keep repeating.

Once the loop ends, the variable n is converted into a string and returned.

Step 6: Output the Padlock Combination

After all characters have been processed, the program outputs the padlockCombination.

Problem 19 – Reading The Rules

Example Solution:

```
DECLARE rulesFile : FILE
DECLARE line : STRING

OPENFILE rulesFile FOR READ
"UltimateGameRules.txt"

REPEAT
    READFILE rulesFile, line
    IF NOT EOF(rulesFile) THEN
        OUTPUT line
    ENDIF
UNTIL EOF(rulesFile)

CLOSEFILE rulesFile
```

Step-by-Step Explanation:

Step 1: Declare Variables and Arrays

The algorithm uses two variables. The variable `line` is a string that will hold each line of the text file to output, and `rulesFile` which uses a data type of FILE. This is a special data type for holding the contents of the text file.

Step 2: Open the File for Reading

The Algorithm opens the file "UltimateGameRules.txt" for reading. This file contains the secret rules for the ultimate game Alex and Jordan have prepared. The `OPENFILE` command is used to access the file and READ allows the algorithm to get the data from the file.

Step 3: Read the File Contents

The algorithm uses a REPEAT UNTIL loop that will repeat until it reaches the end of the file (EOF, which stands for End Of File). Inside the loop, the READFILE command reads one line from the file at a time and stores it in the variable called `line`.

Step 4: Output Each Line

After each line is read, the algorithm checks with an IF statement to ensure it hasn't reached the end of the file. If it's not at the end, it outputs the line read from the file.

Step 5: Close the File

Once the end of the file is reached, the loop ends and the algorithm closes the file with the CLOSEFILE command. It's important to close the file as it's locked and can't be used for anything else until it's closed.

Problem 20 – The Guest List

Example Solution:

```
DECLARE guestFile : FILE
DECLARE guestName : STRING

OPENFILE guestFile FOR WRITE
"CelebrationGuestList.txt"

REPEAT
    OUTPUT "Enter a guest's name (or type 'END' to finish):"
    INPUT guestName
    IF guestName <> "END" THEN
        WRITEFILE guestFile, guestName
    ENDIF
UNTIL guestName = "END"
```

Step-by-Step Explanation:

Step 1: Declare Variables and Arrays

The algorithm uses two variables. The variable `guestName` is a string that will hold the names that Alex or Jordan input, and `guestFile` which uses a data type of FILE. Just like before, this is a special data type for holding the contents of the text file.

Step 2: Open the File for Writing

The algorithm opens "CelebrationGuestList.txt" for writing by using the OPENFILE command with the key word WRITE. This action creates the file if it doesn't exist or clears it if it already does, preparing it to store the guest list.

Step 3: Input Guest Names

Using a REPEAT UNTIL loop, the algorithm prompts Alex, Jordan, or any user to enter a guest's name. This allows the user to keep entering as many names as they want to.

Step 4: Write Names to the File

Still inside the loop, before writing the name to the file, an IF statement checks if the entered name is not "END". If they haven't typed in "END", the WRITEFILE command writes the entered name to the file, adding each guest to the guest list.

Step 5: Ending the Loop

The loop continues until the word "END" is entered as the guest name. This string is a signal to stop entering names and finish the loop.

Step 6: Close and Save the File

Finally, the CLOSEFILE command is used to close the file. This action closes the file for other programs to use, but also saves the data to the file – without closing, the file won't be saved!

Extra Challenge Solution:

The Digital Invitation Challenge

Example Solution:

```
DECLARE guestList : ARRAY [0..2][0..10] OF STRING
DECLARE gameOptions : ARRAY OF STRING
DECLARE name, favoriteGame : STRING
DECLARE age, i, maxIndex, position : INTEGER
DECLARE done, gameValid : BOOLEAN
DECLARE topGames : ARRAY [0..2] OF STRING


gameOptions ← [["Chess","5"], ["Monopoly","3"],
["Scrabble","4"], ["Catan","2"], ["Risk","1"],
["Ticket to Ride","2"], ["Carcassonne","0"],
["Pandemic","2"]

done ← FALSE

REPEAT
    OUTPUT "Enter your name (type 'done' to finish):"
    INPUT name
    IF name = "done" THEN
        done ← TRUE
    ENDIF

    WHILE name = "" THEN
        OUTPUT "Name cannot be blank. Please enter a valid name."
        INPUT name
    END WHILE
```

```
    OUTPUT "Enter your age:"
    INPUT age


   WHILE age < 11 OR age > 17
        OUTPUT "Invalid age. Please enter an age
between 11 and 17."
        INPUT age
    END WHILE

    gameValid ← TRUE
    REPEAT
        OUTPUT "Select your favourite game
(number):"
        FOR i ← 0 TO LENGTH(gameOptions) - 1 DO
            OUTPUT (i + 1) + ". " +
gameOptions[i]
        NEXT i

        INPUT favoriteGame

        IF NOT (favoriteGame IN gameOptions) THEN
            OUTPUT "Invalid game selection.
Please select a valid game from the list."
            gameValid ← FALSE
        ELSE
            position ←
gamesTally[INDEXOF(gameOptions, favoriteGame)]
            gameOptions[position] ←
gameOptions[position] + 1

        ENDIF
    UNTIL gameValid = TRUE
```

```
        guestList ← guestList + [[name, STRING(age),
favoriteGame]]

UNTIL done = FALSE

// Identify top three games

FOR i ← 1 TO 3 DO
    maxIndex ← INDEXOF(MAX(gamesTally),
gamesTally)
    topGames ← topGames + [gameOptions[maxIndex]]
    gamesTally[maxIndex] ← 0 // Reset this tally
to find the next highest
NEXT i


OUTPUT "Choice 1: " + topGames[0]
OUTPUT "Choice 2: " + topGames[1]
OUTPUT "Choice 3: " + topGames[2]
```

More Books by The Author

Follow My Author Page

GCSE Computer Science 9-1 Complete Visual Notes for OCR

GCSE Computer Science 9-1 Complete Visual Notes for AQA

iGCSE Computer Science 9-1 Complete Visual Notes for CIE

150 Practice Questions for Cambridge IGCSE Computer Science

My Weekly List: A Planner for People Who Love Planning but Rarely Do

Teach All About It : 100 Down-To-Earth Tips For Making The Most Out Of Your Classroom

For more information about Holly's courses and tuition, visit her website at www.TeachAllAboutIt.uk

Printed in Great Britain
by Amazon